学习中文的最简单方法

2

LEI
XIANGJIAN

版权所有。

版权所有©2019 由 Lei Xiangjian

未经出版商书面许可，不得以任何形式或通过电子或机械方式（包括影印，录制或任何信息存储和检索系统）复制或传播本书的任何部分。

此版本包含完整文本

原版精装版。

没有一个字被省略。

学习中文的最简单方法2

一本令人发指的书 发表于

与作者的安排

BAD CREATIVE 出版历史

The Simplest Way To Learn French 2016年3月出版

The Simplest Way To Learn Spanish, 2017年3月出版

即将上市的作品

The Simplest Way To Learn Italian 2, 2019

ISBN: 9781091574496

Vol. 1

Vol. 2

ALSO AVAILABLE IN

- AUDIO
- HARDCOVER
- E-BOOK

FORMATS

有关下一本书的更新，请关注我们
www.facebook.com/BadCreativ3

SOCIAL #TheSimplestWay #LearnChinese2 #BadCreativ3

内容

第1章 - 动词 - 无限

动词 - 完美

动词 - GERUND / FUTURE

动词 - 现在的主旨

动词 - 条件

动词 - 过去的条件

动词 - 过去的主体

第二章 - 被动声音

第3章 - 前提条件

第四章 - 摘要

第五章 - 自然

第六章 - 材料

第七章 - 艺术

第八章 - 措施

第九章 - 医疗

第十章 - 政治

第十一章 - 教育

第十二章 - 不正当行为

第十三章 - 科学

第十四章 - 运输

第十五章 - 经济学

第十六章 - 体育

第十七章 - 精神

第18章 - 调情

第十九章 - 身份

前言

在第一部分中，我们确立了语言是人类状况的一个重要方面的想法，并为您提供了学习一些会话中文的基础知识。 **在第二部分中，我**们通过向您介绍可能以前未涉及的语法的其他方面来扩展这一点。

与其前身一样，本书包含了日常中文对话中一些最常用单词的词典。 **它利用了古老的重复学**习技巧和死记硬背，使大脑尽快学习汉语。 **此外**，还包括一个称为故事模式的辅助功能，以帮助读者进行理解测试。

最后，应该指出的是，虽然本书有助于对汉语单词的视觉识别和理解，但学生也必须理解其正确的发音。 为此，我们将提供随附的有声读物，以便开设听力课程。

因此，**从美**丽的北京城市，爱情之城和时尚之都，我们为您呈现简单的学汉语2。

如何使用本书

1. 这条线是训练线（如果你愿意，可以是T线）

训练时间

它代表了一套二十五个字要记住的结束。

2. 您需要覆盖书的右侧并尝试翻译左侧。
3. **每个正确的翻译都有1分**。在T线之后但不高达25的任何东西都被视为奖金。
4. **在得分至少达到20分之前，不要进入下一批**
5. **故事模式旨在帮助您理解句子中**单词的用法，因此请务必在培训中获得高分，以便充分理解故事。

既然你知道规则，

让我们开始吧。

第1章

动词 - 无限

关键词: Predict, push, know, build, avoid, judge, enter, decrease.

他喜欢建造东西	He likes to build things
很难预测	It is difficult to predict
我要阻止这一点	I am going to prevent that
最好避开那个区域	It is better to avoid that zone
她想见我	She wants to meet me
谢谢你不要推	Thanks for not pushing
你可以看到我感觉很糟糕	I feel bad as you can see
通常，有一些危险的动作要避免	Often, there were dangerous movements to avoid
他们种植水果和蔬菜	They grow fruit and vegetables
一个月后，我可以观察到真正的进展	After one month, I could observe real progress
我喜欢计划用餐	I like to plan meals
我没时间见你	I do not have time to meet you
饭后要避免	To be avoided after meals
我不能动了	I cannot move anymore
你可以输入	You can enter
你不能出去	You cannot go out
我必须寄出信件	I have to send out letters
我要解决这个问题	I am going to resolve the problem

这很难减少	This is hard to decrease
他是谁评判我？	Who is he to judge me?
她打算用苹果填满她的帽子	She is going to fill her hat with apples
她快要出去了	She was about to go out
我可以进来吗？	May I come in?
不，我们将解决这个问题	No, we are going to resolve this
你不能动	You cannot move

训练时间

我有一个小西装盒来填补	I have a small suit case to fill
你可以输入	You can enter
现在判断还为时尚早	It is still too soon to judge
她要保护她的丈夫	She is going to protect her husband
我喜欢运动	I like to exercise
你必须决定	You have to decide
我再也受不了了	I cannot stand it anymore
难以拒绝	Hard to refuse
她没有给我时间思考	She did not give me time to think
我必须提前五分钟	I have to set my watch ahead by five minutes
更换镜子需要多长时？	How much time to replace the mirror?
我今天无法决定	I cannot decide today
我受不了这个声音	I cannot stand this noise

她要保护她的宝宝	She is going to protect her baby
我不想忍受那种噪音	I do not want to put up with that noise
很难描述	It is hard to describe
他们打算关上窗户	They are going to close the window
你可以站起来	You can get up
需要验证此文件	This file needs to be verified
它很容易组织	It will be easy to organize
我要检查一下	I am going to check that
他们要关闭餐厅	They are going to close the restaurant
组织起来并不容易	That is not going to be easy to organize

训练时间

我无法描述这盏灯	I cannot describe this lamp
你打算打破窗户	You are going to break the window
你要检查这辆车	You are going to inspect this car
我不想放弃	I do not want to give up
我想告诉你一切	I want to tell you everything
我认为他会成功	I think he is going to succeed
你必须引用这位作者	You have to cite this author
他们将支持你的努力	They are going to support your efforts
与她交谈毫无用处	It is useless to talk with her

他喜欢讲有趣的故事　　　　　　He likes to tell funny stories
她的儿子肯定会成功　　　　　　Her son is sure to succeed

训练时间

启动汽车　　　　　　　　　　　To start the car
他想花多少钱？　　　　　　　　How much does he want to spend?
他们想收养一个孩子　　　　　　They want to adopt a baby
如果您遇到问题，可以与我联系　You can contact me if you have a problem
我不喜欢用手机　　　　　　　　I do not like to use the phone
我想少花钱　　　　　　　　　　I want to spend less
没有告诉任何人？　　　　　　　Without telling anyone?
我喜欢遛狗　　　　　　　　　　I like to walk my dog
他们可以返回法国　　　　　　　They can return to France
我没有什么可隐藏的　　　　　　I have nothing to hide
我可以接受这辆车了　　　　　　I can accept the car
你将把蛋糕分成四份　　　　　　You will divide the cake into four
我不能接受这项工作　　　　　　I cannot accept this work
我要警告你的父亲　　　　　　　I am going to warn your father
我喜欢躲起来　　　　　　　　　I like to hide
你现在可以转身　　　　　　　　You can turn around now
我要和你分享这个时刻　　　　　I am coming to share this moment with you
她会接受　　　　　　　　　　　She is going to accept

她要为她的丈夫辩护	She is going to defend her husband
你会继续吃	You will continue eating
他很快就会开始	He is going to start soon
我可以借给你我的车	I can lend you my car
一个小机器人来拯救他们	A little robot comes to save them
我想借这本书	I want to borrow this book
那可以从现在开始	That can start now

训练时间

我们必须继续！	We have to continue!
我来救你的猫	I am coming to save your cat
我们想保护动物	We want to protect the animals
你可以把笔借给我吗？	Can you lend me your pen?
我想我已经读过了	I think I have read that
我必须在午夜之前回来	I have to come back before midnight
我不确定我是否喜欢他的主意	I am not sure I liked his idea
你认为你及时完成了？	Do you think you have finished in time?
他似乎完成了他的工作	He seems to have finished his work
我母亲说她喜欢她的礼物	My mother said she liked her present
他不能读这本书	He cannot have read this book
他们说他们去年结婚了	They say they got married last year
我们很高兴我们来了	We are happy that we came

故事模式

ENGLISH

Zhu: "Why do you have to leave? I'm going to miss you a lot."

Ma: "I'm going to miss you too, but there's no need to worry because we'll always be together, no matter where I go, I'll skype you every week."

Zhu: "My birthday is coming soon, and I'm not sure If I can be without you, I want to share this moment with you, my love, I'll ask for a transfer as soon as possible."

Ma: "No problem my love, but the distance between here and my new school is very far."

Zhu: "Do you intend to replace me so soon?"

Ma: "Of course not, how can I?"

Zhu: "So let me be the judge of distance, because my heart is really connected to yours now."

Ma: "It's good, you can come, but be sure to divide the cake into four parts, because I'm going to have two roommates at my new destination."

CHINESE

Zhu: "你为什么要离开？我会很想你的。"

Ma: "我也会想念你，但没有必要担心因为我们永远在一起，无论我走到哪里，我都会每周给你打电话。"

Zhu: "我的生日快到了，我不确定如果没有你，我想和你分享这个时刻，我的爱，我会尽快请求转移。"

Ma: "我的爱没问题，但这里和我的新学校之间的距离很远。"

Zhu: "你打算这么快换掉我吗？"

Ma: "当然不是，我怎么能这样？"

Zhu: "所以让我成为距离的判断者，因为我的心脏现在与你的心脏有关。"

Ma: "这很好，你可以来，但一定要将蛋糕分成四个部分，因为我将在我的新目的地有两个室友。"

动词 - 完美

关键词: Last, added, used, accepted.

我加了牛奶	I had added milk
我认识她的堂兄	I had known her cousin
你已经接受了	You had accepted that
他曾经使用过的物品	The objects that he had used
她给了我茶	She had offered me tea
她得到了什么结果？	What results had she got?
我们接受了它	We had accepted it
他们加了他的名字	They had added his name
这些是您获得的文件	These are the documents that you had obtained
她认识她的叔叔	She had known her uncle
我们回到了法国	We had returned to France
我打电话给医生	I had called the doctor
后来，你来了	Later, you had come
我过去了	I had passed by here
她保持安静	She had kept quiet
这是我们称之为的少年	This is the teenager that we had called

故事模式

ENGLISH

Boss: "I wrote a letter yesterday, if only you had been there, you would have seen it."

Huang: "Once Mrs. Carew offered me tea, it meant I had to listen to one of her terribly long stories, so I left the building at the slightest opportunity."

Boss: "That's right, I guess ... Once she's started, you can never stop her ... Anyway, how are you?" I noticed that you keep going early and late in recent days."

Huang: "All is well sir, I just passed the Simpleway certification exams, with the translation work I have to do here, I only had time at the beginning and end of the shifts to study."

Boss: "Splendid, you know, that's another good idea that you brought to this company, if I knew earlier, I would have given you more free time, it's a useful certification, and must add this publishing house."

Huang: "I'm honored sir, so am I going to have a salary increase for that?"

Boss: "No, not yet, but it's coming soon, rest assured."

CHINESE

老板:"我昨天写了一封信,只要你去过那里,你就会看到它。"

黄:"一旦卡鲁夫人给我提供茶,这意味着我必须听一个她非常长的故事,所以我稍稍离开了大楼。"

老板:"那是对的,我想……一旦她开始,你就永远不能阻止她……无论如何,你好吗?"我注意到你最近几天一直都很早就走了。"

黄:"一切都很好先生,我刚刚通过了Simpleway认证考试,我必须在这里完成翻译工作,我只有时间在轮班的开始和结束时才能学习。"

老板:"太棒了,你知道,这是你带给这家公司的另一个好主意,如果我早些时候知道,我会给你更多的空闲时间,这是一个有用的认证,并且必须加上这个出版社。"

黄:"我很荣幸先生,所以我会加薪吗?"

老板:"不,还没有,但它即将到来,

动词 - GERUND / FUTURE

关键词: Rest, saying, acting.

他会像那样杀了我们	He is going to kill us by acting like that
小时候，他很苗条	As a child, he was rather slim
他离开说好话	He left saying nice things
这样做，人们使用更少的水	In doing so, people use less water
一个人在害怕死亡的时候不能活下去	One cannot live while being afraid of dying
话虽这么说，你是对的	That being said, you are right
人们通过共同行动更有效	People were more effective by acting together
鉴于你的病情，你需要休息一下	Given your condition, you need some rest
通过这样说，你可以获得他们的信任	By saying that, you may gain their trust
我明天不会有空	I will not be free tomorrow
明天会很好	It will be nice tomorrow
没有什么可看的	There will be nothing to see
他们将能够喝酒	They will be able to drink
所以我将不得不做出选择	So I will have to make a choice

训练时间

故事模式

ENGLISH

"Are you having fun?" asked the park guide.

"Being here has always been on my list of things to do, so of course I am. For me, the action is always better than what is said, so I will show what I feel with a backflip." said Chang.

Chang's breathing was hard after the flips. He had not exercised for a long time, and that had an obvious effect on him.

"We at Simpleland, Paris, are happy to be part of your joy, sir, how can we help you?" The guide replied, while squeezing both hands together.

"Well, making a movie and skydiving are also at the top of the list." said Chang.

"Parachuting is pretty risky, but where I come from, we have a saying, 'We can not live when we are afraid of death.'" "Maybe our mountain experience is a good substitute for the fun you're looking for." said the guide.

"That will do for now. Where is it?" Chang asked.

"There in the west, sir." the guide pointed.

- oo O oo –

Barrister Lin: "These are the conditions of your parole, as delivered by Justice Ying."

1. "You will still need to have this anklet on you, so we can track your movements during the parole period."

2. "You will not, or will attempt to do anything that could constitute a public nuisance, within the time limit of your parole."

3. "You will return to the perimeter of the assigned premises at the time prescribed by your Parole Officer."

4. "Any violation of the aforementioned rules means that we will have to revoke your bond, and you will be sent back to prison."

Barrister Lin: "Are the terms clear to you?"

Zhi Wei: "Yes sir, understood."

Barrister Lin: "Good. Now try to stay out of trouble."

CHINESE

"你玩得开心吗?"公园导游问道。

"在这里一直都是我要做的事情,所以我当然也是。 对我来说,动作总是好于所说的,所以我会用后空翻显示我的感受。"张说。

翻转后,张的呼吸很难。 他没有锻炼很长时间,这对他有明显的影响。

"我们在巴黎的Simpleland,很高兴能成为你的快乐的一部分,先生,我们怎么能帮到你?"导游回答说,同时将双手挤在一起。

"好吧, 制作电影和跳伞也是最重要的。"张说。

"跳伞是非常危险的，但是我来自哪里，我们有一句话，'当我们害怕死亡时，我们不能活下去。'""也许我们的山地体验可以替代你正在寻找的乐趣。"指南说。

"那将是现在。 它在哪里？"张问道。

"在西方，先生。"导游指出。

- oo O oo -

律师林："这是你的假释的条件，由英大法官提供。"

1."**你仍然需要把**这个脚镯放在你身上，所以我们可以在假释期间追踪你的动作。"

2."**在你的假**释期限内，你不会或将会尝试做任何可能构成公害的事情。"

3."**您将在假**释官员规定的时间返回指定场所的周边。"

4."**任何**违反上述规定的行为都意味着我们必须撤销你的保释金，你将被送回监狱。"

Barrister Lin: "你的条款清楚吗？"

Zhi Wei: "是的先生，明白了。"

Barrister Lin: "好。 现在尽量避免麻烦。"

动词 - 现在的主旨

关键词: Although, live, life, react.

即使	Even though
他们有必要看见我的妹妹	It is necessary that they see my sister
你在这里很好	It is good that you are here
他是唯一需要搬家的人	He is the only one who needs to move
看来她无法前来	It seems she is unable to come
我不确定你能从远处看到细节	I am not sure that you can see details from a distance
他必须看到他的儿子	He has to see his son
我希望他们成为我的朋友	I want them to be my friends
她是唯一有车的人	She is the only one who has a car
我们很高兴他有律师	We are glad that he has a lawyer
他们有必要看到我们的堂兄	It is necessary that they see our cousin
西班牙万岁	Long Live Spain
他必须关上窗户	It is necessary he close the window
他们需要认真对待	They need to get serious
我不希望你这样做	I do not want you to do it
她这么说很奇怪	It is strange for her to say that
她旅行更重要	It is important that she travels more
找工作很重要	It is important that you look for a job

| 她活着很重要 | It is important that she live |

我不确定他是在做他的工作 / I am not sure that he is doing his work

妈妈要你关上窗户 / Mom wants you to close the window

我很高兴你在这个季节旅行 / I am pleased you travel in this season

我很抱歉他们正在关闭商店 / I am sorry that they are closing the store

你住在这里很好 / It is good that you are living here

我们不希望你做出反应 / We do not want you to react badly

这是一个坚固的书包携带 / It is a sturdy bag for carrying your books

他将在夏天到来之前去训练 / He is going to train before the summer comes

他必须快速进入 / It is necessary that he enter quickly

训练时间

故事模式

ENGLISH

Wang: "Even though I often say no, I know it's difficult to find a job in this recession, so in the spirit of brotherhood, I'll leave money to buy food. But I will not always do so. And so you have to find a legal way to make ends meet, and be self-sufficient."

Suzuka: "No problem big brother, thank you."

CHINESE

Wang: "**尽管我**经常说不,但我知道在这次经济衰退中找工作很困难,所以本着兄弟情谊的精神,我会留下钱买菜。 **但我不会一直**这样做。 因此,**你必须找到一种合法的方式来**维持生计,并且自给自足。"

Suzuka: "**大哥没**问题,谢谢。"

动词 - 条件

关键词: Could, should.

有人会说他很有钱	One would say that he is rich
没有它，我会是对的	Without it, I would be right
你应该睡觉，我的儿子	You should sleep, my son
他会成为一个好丈夫	He would make a good husband
我们现在应该吃	We should eat now
我想我们可以成为好朋友	I think that we could be good friends
你能为爱做什么？	What would you be able to do for love?
我应该去睡觉了	I should go to bed
我们会拥有它	We would have it
可能有三个或四个	There might be three or four of them
我会说你二十岁	I would say that you are twenty
如果我身体健康，我会很高兴	If I were in good health, I would be happy
没有其他人可以做我的工作	No other man could do my work
我的朋友们想去	My friends would like to go
那个女人会去法国	That woman would be going to France
我想吃	I would like to eat

她想睡觉	She would like to sleep
我们不知道我们的女儿是否会喜欢这个主意	We don't know if our daughter would like this idea
你想去	You would like to go
我想喝牛奶	I would like to drink milk
我们想和你的学生说英语	We would like to speak English with your students
你想吃同样的东西吗？	Would you like to eat the same thing?
马和黄想去非洲	Ma and Huang would like to go to Africa
我不是一只鸟，但我想成为一只鸟	I am not a bird, but I would like to be one
如今，她肯定会入狱	Nowadays, she would certainly go to jail

训练时间

故事模式

ENGLISH

Mr. Fen: "Young man, you look stressed, is everything okay?"

Young boy on the bridge: "I know; I would go so far as to say that I am depressed."

Mr. Fen: "It's not good to hear, any reasons in particular?"

Young Boy: "That." he said, handing a brown envelope to Mr Fen.

Mr. Fen: "What is it?"

Young Boy: "A list of things I had hoped to accomplish at this stage of my life."

Mr. Fen: "I see, how old are you?"

Young Boy: "Guess."

Mr. Fen: "I would say that you are seventeen or eighteen years old."

Young Boy: "If you say seventeen, you would be right. I could read them out loud if you want to hear."

Mr. Fen: "Of course, go ahead, I'm intrigued."

Young Boy: "Number one: At the age of eighteen, I would make a name for myself."

"Number 2. At the age of eighteen, I would go to France or a French-speaking country for a year."

"Number 3. At the age of eighteen, I would have made my first million."

That's it for now, my birthday is next week, and I'm still updating the list."

Mr. Fen: "You are either a joker, or you worry unnecessarily: many of us have objectives that we will never reach in life. Many of us do not have a million or even a thousand."

Young Boy: "But most of the items on my list depend on number three."

Mr. Fen: "Well, now that you know what to focus on, start working, things will be clearer and better, trust me."

Young Boy: "Thanks for the chat, I needed that."

CHINESE

Mr. Fen: "年轻人，你看起来很紧张，一切都好吗？"

Young boy on the bridge: "我知道;我甚至会说我很沮丧。"

Mr. Fen: "听到这个，特别是任何理由都不好听？"

Young Boy: "那个。"他说，把一个棕色信封递给了Fenie先生。

Mr. Fen: "它是什么？"

Young Boy: "我希望在我生命的这个阶段完成的事情清单。"

Mr. Fen: "我明白了，你多大了？"

Young Boy: "猜猜想。"

Mr. Fen: "我会说你十七岁或十八岁。"

Young Boy: "如果你说十七岁，你就是对的。如果你想听，我可以大声读出来。"

Mr. Fen: "当然，继续吧，我很感兴趣。"

Young Boy: "第一：十八岁时，我会为自己起个名。"

"2号。在十八岁的时候，我会去法国或法语国家一年。"

"数字3.在十八岁的时候，我会成为我的第一个百万。"

这就是现在，我的生日是下周，我还在更新清单。"

Mr. Fen: "你要么是一个小丑，要么你不必要地担心：我们中的许多人都有我们永远无法实现的目标。我们中的许多人没有一百万甚至一千。"

Young Boy: "但我名单上的大多数项目都依赖于第三名。"

Mr. Fen: "好吧，既然你知道要关注什么，开始工作，事情会更清晰，更好，相信我。"

Young Boy: "谢谢你的聊天，我需要那个。"

动词 – 过去的条件

关键词: Recognized, watched, offered, detained.

他会阻止我们	He would have stopped us
你会去市政厅	You would have gone to the city hall
不，这会更糟	No, this would have been worse
她会认出你的车	She would have recognized your car
我们一起去商店	We would have gone to the store together
我们已经准备好了	We would have been ready
没有它，我们就会认出你	Without that, we would have recognized you
那些话应该是我的最后一句话	Those words would have been my last
我相信你会成为一名非常优秀的医生	I am sure that you would have been a very good physician
你会去乡村学校	You would have gone to the village school
你会少付钱	You would have paid less
她会强调这一点	She would have emphasized that
我本来会放一个节目	I would have presented a show
放学后我们会看电视	We would have watched television after school
他给了我们一杯饮料	He'd have offered us a drink

故事模式

ENGLISH

Stranger 1: "I hate to say it, but I told you so.

I specifically insisted on the words 'do not look at him', he would have offered to buy us a drink, or you would have at least paid less."

Zhi Wei: "I'm sorry, there is still time, we can still go back."

Stranger 1: "There is no reason to, they would have already looked at the tapes. You showed fear. You were not ready to become this person when it was most needed.

"It was a good thing that we stopped when we did, otherwise we would have suffered the consequences of being captured again."

Zhi Wei: "Once again, I'm sorry."

CHINESE

Stranger 1: "**我不想**这么说,但我告诉你了。

我特意坚持"**不要看他**"这个词,他会提出给我们买一杯饮料,否则你至少会少付钱。"

Zhi Wei: "**我很抱歉,**还有时间,我们仍然可以回去。"

Stranger 1: "**没有理由,他们**已经看过录像带了。**你表**现出恐惧。**在最需要的**时候,你还没准备好成为这个人。

"**当我**们这样做时,我们就停止了这是一件好事,否则我们会遭受再次被捕的后果。"

Zhi Wei: "**再一次,我很抱歉。**"

动词 - 过去的主体

关键词: Eaten, too much, had, lost.

我们很高兴您越过了边境	We are happy that you have crossed the border
我认为她没有准备好这个阶段	I do not think she prepared this stage
好像她生病了	It seems like she has been sick
这是她拥有的最漂亮的衣服	It is the most beautiful dress that she has had
这些是对我们很好的唯一男人	These are the only men that have been nice to us
这是我很久以来见过的最英俊的男人	This is the most handsome man I have seen in a long time
对不起，你错过了会议	I am sorry that you missed the meeting
我不确定你吃饱了	I am not sure you have had enough to eat
我不认为马等了太久	I do not think Ma waited too long
似乎他们更精确	It seems that they have been more precise
看来她生病了	It seems that she has been sick
你去巴黎很棒	It is great that you have gone to Paris
我们喜欢她去博物馆的想法	We like the idea that she went to the museum
我们去动物园很好	It is good that we have gone to the zoo

丈夫有可能在妻子面前归来吗？	Is it possible that the husband returned before his wife?
我不明白我的侄女留在了花园里	I did not understand that my niece had stayed in the garden
他们的母亲担心他们没穿外套就出去了	Their mother is afraid that they have gone out without their coats
妈妈很高兴我们这么早就回来了	Mom was happy that we had returned so early
她最好在家中去世	It was better for her to have died at home
你先走了是合乎逻辑的	It is logical that you have gone first
我怀疑他完成了他的工作	I doubted that he had finished his work
当你接受这个提议时，我很高兴	I was delighted when you accepted the offer
他离开时我很高兴	I was happy when he left
我确信他会开车	I was sure that he would drive
我希望他能在车站看到这辆车	I wanted him to see the car at the station

训练时间

故事模式

ENGLISH

"My God, what has happened here?" asked the detective.

"She died this morning, she was diabetic." Hiro said.

He pointed a picture of the deceased on the wall.

"I thought she went to the doctor this week." said Detective Guo.

"Nobody really knows much, she just came in, she fell to the ground, and that was all. But it's possible that it was a bad diagnosis, it looked very serious.

Also, the family started a protest, destroying everything in sight, claiming we had not done enough. We could sue them, but the legal process would be long, and I'm not really interested."

"We will discuss it later. For now, we will find out more." said the detective.

CHINESE

"**我的上帝，这里发生了什么？**"侦探问道。

"**她今天早上去世，她患有糖尿病。**"希罗说。

他在墙上指着死者的照片。

"**我以**为她这周去了医生。"郭侦探说。

"**没有人真正知道，她**刚进来，她倒在地上，就是这样。 但这可能是一个不好的诊断，看起来非常严重。

此外，这个家庭开始抗议，摧毁了一切，声称我们做得还不够。 **我**们可以起诉他们，但法律程序会很长，我真的不感兴趣。"

"**我**们稍后会讨论它。 现在，我们会发现更多。"侦探说。

第二章

被动声音

关键词: Adopted, done, respected, read.

他被他的人民所爱	He is loved by his people
它是由计算机完成的	It is done by computer
他被他们收养了吗？	Has he been adopted by them?
孩子被我的叔叔和姑姑收养了	The child has been adopted by my uncle and my aunt
她深受大家的喜爱	She was loved by everybody
你的床是吗？	Was your bed made?
这只猫被好人收养了	The cat has been adopted by nice people
他被一对夫妇收养	He is adopted by a couple
他受到所有人的尊重	He is respected by all
那份文件是我父亲读过的	That document was read by my father
妻子受到丈夫的尊重	The wife is respected by her husband
古老的传统仍然受到尊重	Old traditions were still respected
该报被广大读者阅读	The newspaper is read by a wide audience

训练时间

故事模式

ENGLISH

Chun: "Do not worry about the marking, everything is done by computer, just have a copy of your credentials. Once my virus reads the password of the registrar, we can change as much as possible."

Bo: "I really respect your hacking abilities."

Chun: "Thanks, and if you like video games, we can play the new Adopted Suns game, or FIFA if you prefer. I have both, we can play all night if you wish."

Bo: "Can I ask something?"

Chun: "Yes, of course."

Bo: "Why didn't we become friends earlier?"

Chun: "I do not know either, my friend, but for now, all roads lead to the playground."

laughs shared

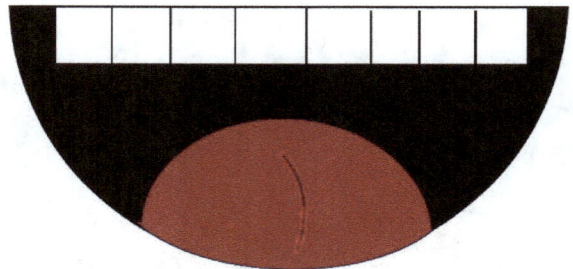

CHINESE

Chun:"**不要担心**标记,一切都是通过计算机完成的,只需要一份你的凭证。 **一旦我的病毒**读取了注册商的密码,我们就可以尽可能地进行更改。"

Bo:"**我真的很尊重你的黑客攻**击能力。"

Chun:"谢谢,如果你喜欢电子游戏,我们可以玩新的Adopted Suns游戏,或者你喜欢的FIFA游戏。 **我有两个,如果你愿意,我们可以整晚玩。**"

Bo:"**我能**问点什么吗?"

Chun:"**是的,当然。**"

Bo:"为什么我们不早点成为朋友?"

Chun:"**我也不知道,我的朋友,**但现在,所有的道路都通往操场。"

笑分享

第3章

前提条件

关键词: Until, in the middle of, outside of, next to, you must.

直到最近	Until recently
我们就在你身边	We are next to you
这座桥就在塔旁边	The bridge is next to the tower
我要去我女儿的家	I am going up to my daughter's house
这是因为这只狼	This is because of this wolf
她和她的孩子很亲近	She is close to her children
到现在为止还挺好	So far, so good
天气很好，直到中午	The weather was fine until noon
因雪而无法工作	He cannot work because of the snow
他住在隔壁	He lives next door
狮子吃到晚上	The lion eats until night
我们认为他们很糟糕	In our opinion, they are bad
我在面包店前面	I am in front of the bakery
你在跟我说什么？	What are you saying to me?
她在她房间的中间发现了一只老鼠	She found a mouse in the middle of her room
城外有一家新公司	There is a new company outside the city
你必须靠近你的母亲	You have to stay close to your mother
据我的妻子说，是的	According to my wife, yes

我正在读一本英文杂志	I am reading an English magazine
两兄弟正在屋外玩耍	The two brothers are playing outside the house
我吃了很多肉	I eat a lot of meat
这超出了我的力量	It is beyond my strength
他走过他的卧室	He walks through his bedroom

训练时间

它位于建筑物的顶部	It is on top of the building
你办公桌下有什么东西？	What is there under your desk?
他喝了很多啤酒	He drinks a lot of beer
猫在塔的脚下	The cat is at the foot of the tower
我在外套下面穿夹克	I wear a jacket underneath my coat
我有很多书	I have a lot of books
她把钥匙放在盒子上面	She put the key above the box
她看透了窗帘	She sees through the drapes
您必须在页面底部写下您的名字	You have to write your name at the bottom of the page

训练时间

故事模式

ENGLISH

Bo: "I do not know how I'm going to get by. Thanks to him, I could not get ready in time."

Suzuka: "How about sitting by the window?"

Bo: "It's beyond me, I will not be able to see much."

Suzuka: "And if you sit in front of her, next to the Asian?"

Bo: "It's as good as the examiner sitting on my head, and the Asian does not score as many points in the tests as the girl in blue."

Patrick: "You do not have to worry about anything, all exams can be passed if you have the right knowledge."

Bo: "What are you talking about?"

Patrick: "From what I've heard, the examiner does not oppose handkerchiefs, just write a few points on one and read them under your desk."

CHINESE

Bo: "我不知道自己会怎么样。多亏了他,我无法及时做好准备。"

Suzuka: "坐在窗边怎么样?"

Bo: "这超出了我,我将无法看到太多。"

Suzuka: "如果你坐在她面前,在亚洲人旁边?"

Bo: "就像坐在我头上的考官一样好,亚洲人在考试中得分不如蓝色女孩那么多。"

Patrick: "你不必担心任何事情,如果你有正确的知识,所有的考试都可以通过。"

Bo: "你在说什么?"

Patrick: "从我所听到的情况来看,审查员并不反对手帕,只需在一个上写几个点,然后在你的桌子下阅读。"

第四章

摘要

关键词: Benefits, preparation, network, personality, shock, identity, duty, maximum, minimum.

关键是准备	The key is preparation
这是一个谜	It is a mystery
网络非常大	The network is very big
我妈妈需要休息	My mother needs rest
他耽搁了	He arrived with delay
每个词都有其含义	Each word has its meaning
这是件坏事	It is a bad piece
我很抱歉迟到了	I am sorry for being late
这是一个老技巧	It is an old trick
他没有反应	He has no reaction
他承担责任	He bears responsibility
有什么好处？	What are the advantages?
这个命题很有意思	The proposition is interesting
完美的搭配	The perfect mix
他们想加薪	They want a raise
好处很少	The benefit is little
公众的反应是积极的	The public's reactions are positive
它是混合颜色	It is a mix of colors
结论	The conclusion
她没有个性	She has no personality
这是免费的	Its entry is free
他很震惊	He is in shock

这是一种保护手段	It is a means of protection
那个人害怕改变	That man is afraid of change
他终于失去了审判	He finally loses the trial

训练时间

他们为什么要这些改变？	Why do they want those changes?
太遗憾了！	What a pity!
该计划不再存在	That programme does not exist any more
这是我的身份证	It is my identity card
你喜欢开会	You like meetings
这是你的职责	That is your duty
这个词来自法国	That word is of French origin
那次会议很漫长	That meeting was very long
我有很多功课要做	I have a lot of homework to do
这辆车有很多损坏	The car has a lot of damage
这是重要的一步	It is an important step
光明	The light
我没有太多选择	I do not have many options
我必须检查我的日程安排	I have to check my schedule
谢谢你的邀请	Thanks for your invitation
你没帮我	You do not help me
我需要休息一下	I need a break
我更喜欢这个版本	I prefer this version
我喜欢这个选项	I like that option
我打开灯	I turn on the light

谢谢您的帮助	Thank you for your help
存在多个版本	Several versions exist
灯是红色的	The lights are red
我需要帮助	I need help

训练时间

这是一个久违的	It is a long absence
我的名字可以在列表中找到	My name can be found in the list
多少个类别？	How many categories?
他的父亲有联系	His father has connections
我想要两个孩子	I want two children maximum
我每天工作至少八小时	I work a for a minimum of eight hours a day
我属于同一类别	I am in the same category
我对他们的关系一无所知	I do not know anything about their relationship
我在这里参加会议	I am here for the conference
她接受了良好的教育	She received a good education
她已将此案告上法庭	She has taken the case to court
这个男人状况不佳	This man is in bad shape

故事模式

ENGLISH

Barrister Lin: "What a pity, the news of his imprisonment shocked me. This program already existed for people with bad personalities, which means that I still have to watch him, even if he loses this case."

Stranger 1: "What are our options now?"

Barrister Lin: "Fortunately for us, he has forged cordial relationships over the years with influential people from the Department of Education, some of whom are on the jury today, which means we can benefit from familiarity.

Although this is insignificant in the grand scheme of things, it is nevertheless an advantage, and we need all the little ones we can get. The lights are green for us in this case, and I think the good mix of factual evidence and compassion will take us somewhere."

Stranger 1: "It's good to hear."

Barrister Lin: "We'll talk more after the break ... For now, let's go to the staff bar for some food."

Stranger 1: "Is it cheaper there?"

Barrister Lin: "We have nothing to pay, admission is free on Thursdays."

CHINESE

Barrister Lin: "真可惜,他被监禁的消息震惊了我。这个程序已经存在于性格不好的人身上,这意味着我仍然需要看他,即使他失去了这个案子。"

Stranger 1: "我们现在有什么选择?"

Barrister Lin: "对我们来说幸运的是,他多年来与教育部的有影响力的人建立了亲密的关系,其中一些人今天在评委会上,这意味着我们可以从熟悉中受益。

虽然这在宏观计划中微不足道,但它仍然是一个优势,我们需要所有我们能得到的小孩。在这种情况下,我们的灯光是绿色的,我认为事实证据和同情的良好组合将把我们带到某个地方。"

Stranger 1: "很高兴听到。"

Barrister Lin: "休息后我们会谈更多……现在,我们去工作人员吧寻找食物吧。"

Stranger 1: "那里更便宜吗?"

Barrister Lin: "我们无需支付任何费用,周四免费入场。"

第五章

自然

关键词： Mountain, sun, fire, sky, sea, nature, air, elements, ground, forest, grass, moon, smoke.

火	Fire
太阳	The sun
植物	The plant
风	The wind
元素	The element
一颗树	A tree
太阳在天空中	The sun is in the sky
她看到了大海	She sees the sea
自然是我们的母亲	Nature is our mother
我们的水没有受到污染	Our water is not polluted
这里的空气很纯净	The air is pure here
灯是红色的	The light is red
天是蓝的	The sky is blue
大海是蓝色的	The sea is blue
我喜欢他的花	I like his flowers
他睡在地上	He sleeps on the ground
这个物种已经消失了	The species has disappeared
这些字段是黄色的	The fields are yellow
本正在上阵	Ben is on the wave
玫瑰	Roses
我们的草是绿色的	Our grass is green
狼在森林里	The wolf is in the forest
我不喜欢下雨	I do not like rain
我看到了月亮	I see the moon
我喜欢热量	I like the heat

| 在那个国家，雨很少见 | Rain is rare in that country |
| 她看着山 | She looks at the mountain |

训练时间

河流	The rivers
种子	Seeds
星球	The planet
雪	The snow
峰会在哪里？	Where is the summit?
景观	The landscape
它不是明星	It is not a star
烟是白色的	The smoke is white
这条河很危险	The river is dangerous
景观很棒	The landscape is wonderful
它闻起来像烟雾	It smelled like smoke
这个星球处于危险之中	The planet is in danger
海洋是蓝色的	The ocean is blue
湖很深	The lake is very deep
气候非常好	The climate is very nice
云是白色的	The cloud is white
有污染	There is pollution
这对环境有益	It is good for the environment
电是非常有用的	Electricity is very useful
它开始下雪了	It started to snow

故事模式

ENGLISH

Mei: "Thanks for the flowers, I've been looking for this particular species everywhere."

Ju: "Really, it's great because I brought enough for you to grow a forest."

Mei: "Unfortunately, it would be totally impossible to do here."

Ju: "Why do you say that?"

Mei: "Personal experience. Plant species will never survive in this climate. There were okra seeds I bought last year, six months later, none of them survived."

Ju: "It's unfortunate."

Mei: "Yes, and it's like that for several reasons: first, it's almost always raining, so this place is ridiculously cold all year long … Secondly, the soil is just not good enough."

Ju: "So why do you choose to live in such an environment?"

Mei: "The air is cleaner, with less traffic and industrial activity. When it stops raining, the birds whisper softly in the morning through my window and build nests with beautiful eggs inside."

Ju: "I see."

CHINESE

Mei: "谢谢花儿,我一直在寻找这个特殊的物种。"

Ju: "**真的**, 这很棒,因为我为你带来了足够的森林。"

Mei: "**不幸的是**, 这里完全不可能。"

Ju: "**你**为什么这么说?"

Mei: "**个人经历**。 **植物物种永**远不会在这种气候下生存。 **我去年**购买了秋葵种子,六个月后,他们都没有活下来。"

Ju: "这很不幸。"

Mei: "**是的**, **就像**这样,有几个原因:首先,它几乎总是在下雨,所以这个地方整年都是非常冷的……**其次**, **土壤**还不够好。"

Ju: "**那么你**为什么选择在这样的环境中生活呢?"

Mei: "**空气更清洁**,交通和工业活动减少。 **当它停止下雨时**,鸟儿在早晨通过窗户轻轻地低语,并在里面筑巢,里面有美丽的鸡蛋。"

Ju: "**我明白了**。"

第六章

材料

关键词: Wood, oil, silver, leather, gold.

冰块	The ice
石头	The stone
黄金	The gold
木头	The wood
论文	The paper
她有很多钱	She has a lot of money
那把刀是铁制的	That knife is made of iron
我喜欢冰	I like ice
这是黄金	This is gold
请你的论文	Your papers, please
那座桥是用石头砌成的	That bridge is made of stone
那个盒子是纸制的	That box is made of paper
门由钢制成	The door is made of steel
硬币由金属制成	Coins are made of metal
美国富含石油	America is rich in oil
灰尘在地板上	The dust is on the floor
这种塑料是绿色的	This plastic is green
羊毛质量很好	The wool is of good quality
我不喜欢塑料	I do not like plastic
这只猫带走了我的羊毛	This cat has taken my wool
它像灰尘一样干燥	It is dry as dust

故事模式

ENGLISH

Gold, iron, oil, cotton, rubber. What do these five have in common? If you guessed they are all raw materials, then you would be right.

Raw materials are often natural substances that can be turned into new products through processing activities. Do not believe me? Look around you. The coins are metal. Your belts are leather. The forks and spoons you eat with, are mainly silver. Wood is another good example of raw material. After the treatment, the sawdust can also be used as raw material in the creation of another product.

CHINESE

金，铁，油，棉，橡胶。 这五个有什么共同之处？ 如果您猜到它们都是原材料，那么您就是对的。

原材料通常是天然物质，可以通过加工活动转化为新产品。 不相信我？ 看看你周围。 硬币是金属的。 你的皮带是皮革。 你吃的叉子和勺子主要是银。 木材是另一个原料的好例子。 在处理之后，锯末也可以用作另一种产品的原料。

第七章

艺术

关键词: Painting, music, poetry, artist, film, novel.

电影院	The theater
电影	The movie
小提琴	The violin
这首诗	The poem
节奏	The rhythm
艺术家	The artist
艺术	The arts
博物馆	The museum
歌手	The singer
这个仪器	The instrument
这是一个音符	It is a musical note
你有这幅画	You have the painting
它今年流行	It is in fashion this year
我不**喜**欢这种表现	I have not liked this performance
这是一个伟大的作品	It is a great piece
他的成绩非常好	His marks are excellent
我在看阿姨的作品	I am looking at my aunt's works
今年的时装完全不同	This year's fashions are completely different
你有油漆	You have the paint
他是一个活着的作家吗？	Is he a living writer?

我想去电影院	I want to go to the cinema
他们是艺术家	They are artists
有时，他们背诵诗歌	Sometimes, they recite poems
它用于看电影	It is used for watching movies
博物馆在哪里？	Where is the museum?

训练时间

现场	The scene
我戴着面具	I wear a mask
设计不同	The design is different
这幅画在哪里？	Where is the painting?
这是我的小说	It is for my novel
我听歌	I listen to songs
他喜欢钢琴	He likes the piano
她去过那场音乐会	She has gone to that concert
我想要一把吉他	I want a guitar
演员与国王说话	The actor speaks with the king
他是歌手	He is a singer
演员们	The actors
我们的儿子有三把吉他	Our son has three guitars
明喜欢听小提琴	Ming likes to listen to the violin
他弹钢琴	He plays the piano
我用相机	I use the camera
我正在开车	I am drawing a car
照片很漂亮	The photograph is beautiful

这位音乐家有很多朋友	The musician has a lot of friends
他喜欢文学	He likes the literature
我的叔叔喜欢建筑	My uncle loves architecture
相机	The cameras
他正在拍照	He is taking photographs
两位音乐家正在演出一部着名的作品	The two musicians are playing a famous work

训练时间

这位音乐家正带着她的小提琴来	The musician is coming with her violin
在舞台上	On stage
他不喜欢批评	He does not like criticism
这是一个关于狗的系列	It is a series about a dog
她喜欢写诗	She loves writing poems
我总是唱歌	I always sing
你的话很美	Your words are beautiful
我正在写一首诗	I am writing a poem
鸟儿唱歌	The birds sing
我不是批评家	I am not a critic
她唱得很好	She sings very well
这个系列是最近的	This series is very recent

训练时间

故事模式

ENGLISH

"It's a beautiful painting, I did not know you were artistic:" commented Ma.

"Not as much as you think, but my sister is." Qiang replied.

"She loves drawing, literature and music, and her poetry shows are always filled with rhymes and rhythms, you should see a show when you have the time.

On the other hand, the only artistic thing about me is that I can play both bass and electric guitar, and from time to time, I like to attend one or two dinners to meet real artists."

CHINESE

"这是一幅美丽的画,我不知道你是艺术家:"马云评论道。

"**没有你想象的那么多,但是我的妹妹是。**"Qiang回答道。

"**她喜**欢绘画、文学和音乐,她的诗歌节目总是充满了押韵和节奏,你应该在有空的时候看一场秀。

另一方面,关于我的唯一艺术之处在于我可以演奏低音和电吉他,并且我不时会参加一到两次晚宴以结识真正的艺术家。"

第八章

措施

关键词： Weight, speed, liter, tons, centimeters, kilograms, metric, volume, width, size, height, length.

深度	Depth
高度	Height
一吨一千公斤	There are a thousand kilos in a ton
一米一百厘米	There are one hundred centimeters in one meter
最多有二十公里	There are twenty kilometres at most
我有一升葡萄酒	I have one litre of wine
船的长度非常不同	The lengths of the boats are very different
另一厘米	Another centimeter
他吃了很多鱼	He eats tons of fish
这家人每周喝几升牛奶	The family drinks several litres of milk per week
我家和办公室之间大概有一公里	There is about one kilometer between my house and my office
他吃了三分之一的蛋糕？	He eats one third of the cake?
他想要一半的蛋糕	He wants half of the cake
四是两次两次	Four is two times two
你的体重是多少？	What is your weight?
它的尺寸是多少？	What size is it?
门的宽度是八十厘米	The width of the door is eighty centimeters
深度很重要	The depth is important
你什么尺寸？	What is your size?

你想要我的一半苹果吗？	Do you want half of my apple?
八是两倍四	Eight is two times four
它是一个鸡蛋的大小	It is the size of an egg
在隔壁的房间里	In the next room

训练时间

房间有正方形的形状	The room has the shape of the square
这对我来说都是一样的	It is all the same to me
什么是新的速度？	What is the new speed?
我的酒窖里有三立方米的木柴	My cellar contains three cubic meters of firewood
这些是方面	These are the sides
正方形的边是相等的	The sides of a square are equal
这是一本两卷的小说	It is a novel in two volumes
我家的高度是七米	The height of my house is seven metres

故事模式

ENGLISH

"How fast does the engine run?" asked Professor Makkonen, the silver-haired engineer, while testing his latest invention on the Elysee bridge.

"Nine- and three-square knots." said his assistant, who was holding a large speedometer.

"What are the height and weight requirements for a depth of eight kilometers below sea level?"

"Four tons and ten feet, sir."

"OK, it's good. Now, how much does it weigh compared to the previous one?" Professor Makkonen asked

"It usually depends on its width and the amount of moisture it contains, and on this point, the two are almost equal; sixty-two to sixty-five pounds," the assistant explained.

"Yes, but it consumes a third of the power of its predecessor, but it also has a greater total distance: ninety centimeters to two meters, unlike fifty centimeters to one meter, so there is a difference." said the proffessor.

The assistant took out his notebook and scribbled some figures.

CHINESE

"发动机运转的速度有多快?"银发工程师Makkonen教授在爱丽舍桥上测试他的最新发明时问道。

"九平方和三平方节。"他的助手说,他拿着一个大型车速表。

"海拔8公里深度的高度和重量要求是多少?"

"四吨十英尺,先生。"

"好的,这很好。 现在,与前一个相比,它的重量是多少?"Makkonen教授问道

"**它通常取决于它的**宽度和含有的水分量,在这一点上,两者几乎相等;六十二到六十五磅,"助理解释道。

"是的,但是它消耗了前任的三分之一,但它的总距离也更长:九十厘米到两米,不像五十厘米到一米,所以存在差异。"这位专业人士说道。

助理拿出笔记本,潦草地写了一些数字。

第九章

医疗

关键词: Clinic, patients, doctor, health, operation.

手	The hand
鼻子	The nose
耳朵	The ear
手臂	The arm
眼	The eye
身体	The body
脚	The foot
嘴	The mouth
背部	The back
这些都是我们的头脑	These are our heads
医生	The doctor
他的心脏很糟糕	His heart is bad
他很难找到你	He had a hard time finding you
他们病了	They are sick
她头很小	She has a small head
那是我的手	That is my hand
是坏还是危险？	Is it bad or dangerous?
他们病了	They are sick
她的眼睛是蓝色的	Her eyes are blue
他的嘴很大	He has a big mouth
那不是我的年龄	That is not my age
为什么这个操作？	Why this operation?
我儿子的年龄很小	My son is small for his age
血是红色的	The blood is red
我是否需要动手术？	Do I need an operation?

我们徒步去上班	We go to work on foot
然后她张开嘴	Then she opened her mouth
他有两个左脚	He has two left feet
这是最低年龄	It is the minimum age
她的腿很长	Her legs are long
他的额头很大	His forehead is big
她的嘴唇是蓝色的	Her lips are blue
你的脸红了	Your face is red
我闻到了鼻子的味道	I smell with my nose

训练时间

健康	Health
大脑	The brain
牙医	The dentist
医院	The hospital
颈部	The neck
医生	The doctor
她的皮肤很柔软	Her skin is soft
我有大手指，所以我不能使用小键盘	I have big fingers, so I cannot use a small keyboard
你的额头很烫	Your forehead is hot
她的脸很漂亮	She has a very pretty face
我腿疼了	I have a sore leg
我的皮肤干燥	I have dry skin
那位女士用手指吃着	The lady ate with her fingers
她有两条腿	She has two legs
我用刀切了手指	I cut my finger with a knife
他的皮肤很冷	His skin is cold
孩子正在出牙	The child is teething
她的病很严重	Her illness is serious

风险太大了	The risk is too great
我眼里含着泪水	I have tears in my eyes
我的饮食很难	My diet is hard
我感到脖子上有风	I feel the wind on my neck
一颗牙齿，两颗牙齿	One tooth, two teeth
他正在节食	He is on a diet
我母亲哭了	My mother was in tears

训练时间

他失明了	He lost his sight
他的胸部是红色的	His chest is red
你的喉咙发红	Your throat is red
你哥哥是医生	Your brother is a doctor
他的耳朵疼	His ears hurt
他们俩都是医生	Both of them are doctors
她有病毒	She has a virus
那只老虎皮毛很光泽	That tiger has shiny fur
她是一名医生	She is a medical doctor
患者年纪大了	And the patients are old
骨头是白色的	The bone is white
大脑非常敏感	The brain is very sensitive
我们的病人情况相同	Our patient is in the same condition
医学上做得很糟糕	Medicine is doing badly
我们在药房买药	We buy medicine at the pharmacy
我过得很好	I have a good life
心脏是器官	The heart is an organ

我的肩膀疼痛	I have pain in my shoulder
她打算咨询她的丈夫	She is going to consult her husband
之前，我的脸颊红了	Before, my cheeks were red
我们谈到了我们的生活	We spoke about our lives
你必须服用药物	You must take your medication
我得去药店	I have to go to the pharmacy
这名护士在那家诊所工作	This nurse works in that clinic
抱歉你的脚踝	Sorry for your ankle
我的指甲很短	My nails are short
这种肌肉疼	This muscle hurts
你在睡觉的时候长大	You grow while you sleep
胃是器官	The stomach is an organ
我得去看牙医	I have to see a dentist
孩子正在成长	The child is growing
我必须保护我的脚踝和脚	I have to protect my ankles and my feet
我想他已成为一名护士	I think he has become a nurse

训练时间

故事模式

ENGLISH

Ma: "Why are you out of breath?"

Mei: "I was walking very fast."

Ma: "Why, it's not a good idea, considering your injury."

Mei: "I felt a burning sensation in my chest, so I rushed to the pharmacy for self-treatment."

Ma: "Oh, but when did you become a doctor? and why not go to the hospital instead?"

Mei: "Because I do not like the smell of hospitals, it irritates my nose and bends my stomach ... Moreover, there are so many patients everywhere, and sometimes I'm afraid that there is a virus in the air."

Ma: "I can understand, my uncle continued to say similar things until the operation on his heart last year, he needed a donor organ, but there was none, so now he is dead."

Mei: "You always have a horror story to tell, sorry for your uncle."

Ma: "Sorry for your ankle too, and do not worry, everything will be fine, make sure you take your medicine and stay away from the bikes for a while."

CHINESE

Ma: "你为什么喘不过气来?"

Mei: "我走得很快。"

Ma: "为什么,考虑到你的受伤,这不是一个好主意。"

Mei: "我的胸部感到灼烧,所以我赶到药房进行自我治疗。"

Ma: "哦,但你什么时候成为医生?为什么不去医院呢?"

Mei: "因为我不喜欢医院的气味,它会刺激我的鼻子,让我的肚子弯曲……而且,到处都有很多病人,有时候我担心空气里有病毒。"

Ma: "我能理解,我的叔叔继续说类似的话,直到去年他的心脏手术,他需要一个捐献器官,但没有,所以现在他已经死了。"

Mei: "你总是要讲一个恐怖的故事,对你的叔叔抱歉。"

Ma: "对不起你的脚踝,不用担心,一切都会好的,一定要吃药,远离自行车一段时间。"

第十章

政治

关键词: Democracy, president, budget, power, vote, election, mayor, taxes, law, government.

军队	The army
自由	The liberty
经济	The economy
政府	The government
法律	The law
每个社会都有自己的法律	Each society has its laws
经济发展对该国很重要	Economic development is important for that country
这个国家反对战争	This country is against war
国王有权力吗？	Does the king have power?
这是你的权利	It is your right
你有权利	You have rights
他没有任何权力	He does not have any powers
在所有社会中并非总是如此	This is not always the case in all societies
总统与政府会谈	The president talks to the government
这是一个很好的协议	It is a good agreement
人民党	The party of the people
人们喜欢自由	The people like freedom
他在派对上	He is in a party

经济危机	The economic crisis
安静的革命	The quiet revolution
原因是安全	The reason is security
那是正义吗？	Is that justice?
政策	The policies
她为保卫自己的国家而工作	She works for the defense of her country

训练时间

这是一项政策	It is a policy
安全很重要	Safety is important
发展，正义，自由	Development, justice, freedom
部长今天上午发表了重要讲话	The minister has made a major speech this morning
我们占多数	We are the majority
我们不要暴力	We do not want violence
这是最大的反对党	It is the biggest opposition party
欧洲部长在那里	European ministers are there
它是反对派的一方	It is a party of the opposition
这个国家几乎没有暴力	There is almost no violence in this country
大多数人都害怕	The majority is afraid
这位女士在反对派中	This lady is in the opposition
在那个城市，几乎没有暴力	In that city, there is almost no violence
候选人	The candidates
该组织	The organization

选举是明天	The election is tomorrow
我将成为市长	I am going to be mayor
预算非常重要	The budget is very important
我在这里偿还债务	I am here to pay a debt
冲突持续了三十年	The conflict lasts thirty years
我们有一笔荣誉债务	We had a debt of honor
他是市长吗？	Is he the mayor?
这是正确的策略吗？	Is it the right strategy?
什么是国家？	What is a nation?
市长在市政厅	The mayor is in city hall

训练时间

那件事使他成名	That event made him famous
这是一场战争罪	It is a war crime
我们要纳税	We have to pay tax
国民议会在巴黎举行	The national assembly is in Paris
我必须缴税	I have to pay my taxes
战略将是国家的	The strategies will be national
我知道更快乐的事情	I had known happier events
示威是成功的	The demonstration is a success
没有投票权	There is no vote
他是参议员吗？	Is he a senator?
她已经足够投票了	She is old enough to vote

我们相信民主	We believe in democracy
他在议会里有很多朋友	He has a lot of friends in the parliament
意大利是民主国家	Italy is a democracy
示威已经开始	The demonstration has begun
议会更强大，因此必须更负责任	Parliament is more powerful, it must therefore be more responsible
这是大多数人的投票	This is the vote of the majority
他是参议员	He is a senator
她指挥	She conducts
我们必须为自由而战	We have to fight for our freedom
她经营着她的家人	She runs her family
他正前往巴黎	He is heading for Paris
我无法独自对抗市长的政治	I cannot fight against the mayor's politics all alone
他管理着一家餐馆，受到所有人的尊重	He manages a restaurant and is respected by all

训练时间

故事模式

ENGLISH

"I have never been able to understand the monarchy system of government."said Ma. "Why is there at the same time a king, a prime minister and a president? Does the king have special powers or is he above the law?"

"I do not really understand myself, but I guess the monarch's role is to be the physical manifestation of a country's power, all the work is done by the prime minister or the president." said Mei.

"Speaking of presidents, America has a new one." he said, brandishing a baseball cap with the letters M.A.S.A sewn on it.

"The man has nothing to offer as president, he has no respect for women, and there is no proof that he pays his taxes, he is simply a danger to society." said Mei.

"Yesterday's election was rigged, and if there is justice in this world, it would already be canceled."

"I do not agree; he just had a better strategy." said Ma. "I believe in democracy, which puts power in the votes of the people. The results are the voices of popular opinion. America now has a new direction, which is a revolution against the status quo."

CHINESE

"**我从来没有能够理解**君主制的政府制度。"马云说,"为什么国王,总理和总统同时出现?国王有特殊权力还是凌驾于**法律之上?**"

"**我真的不了解自己,但我**认为君主的角色是成为一个国家权力的物质表现,所有工作都由总理或总统完成。"**梅**说。

"说到总统,美国有一个新的。"**他**说,挥舞着棒球帽,上面刻着字母M.A.S.A。

"这位男士没有什么可以作为总统,他不尊重女性,没有证据证明他缴纳税款,他只是对社会的危险。"**梅**说。

"**昨天的**选举被操纵了,如果在这个世界上有正义,它就已经取消了。"

"**我不同意;他只是有一个更好的策略**。"马云说。 "**我相信民主,它**将权力置于人民的选票之中。结果是民意的声音。美国现在有了一个新的方向,这是一场反对现状的革命。"

第十一章

教育

关键词: Semester, course, school, pencil, lessons, studies, university, concepts, school, students.

学生	The student
学校	The school
图书馆	The library
导演	The director
我在班级	I am in the class
这门课很难	This course is very difficult
这项研究非常重要	This study is very important
他从事教育工作	He works in education
孩子们都是好学生	The children are good students
他不喜欢上学	He has not liked school
他需要完成学业	He needs to complete his studies
学生们正在喝葡萄酒	The students are drinking wine
我得读书了	I have to study
我儿子上中学	My son is in secondary school
她去了两所大学	She goes to two universities
真正的智力锻炼	A true intellectual exercise
这是一个很好的图书馆	This is a good library
我是一名学生	I have been a student
有些学生喝酒	Some students drink wine
我哥哥是学生	My brother is a student

我的计划是在澳大利亚学习	My plan is to study in Australia
我们编写脚本	We write scripts
我丢了铅笔	I have lost my pencil
我们每天有六节课	We have six lessons per day
这种尝试很好	The attempt is good

训练时间

课程	The course
他接受过经典训练	He has had a classical training
这是她的描述	This is her description
这是他的第一个学期	It is his first semester
他正在改进他的台词	He is improving his lines
第二课很容易	The second lesson is very easy
有三十支铅笔和十个孩子	There are thirty pencils and ten children
服务员是初学者	The waiter is a beginner
最后，我通过了考试	Finally, I passed the exam

故事模式

ENGLISH

Bo: "In a way, I knew I would find you in the library."

Mei: "I have to be here. For an extra credit, I signed up for an application development course, which means I have to go through a recommended text called" Application Development Principles "and take a test this week."

Bo: "I see, it's good for you. But i'm tired of school, and it's very likely that I will not go to the next class."

Mei: "We are no longer in high school; every lesson must be taken seriously."

Bo: "Or what?"

Mei: "Is it not obvious? or you'll fail."

Bo: "To be honest, I prefer to run the family business, but my father insists that I have to finish my studies first. Contemporary university education is not very important to me, so I'm really not afraid of an F."

Mei: "I understand where you come from, but I do not agree with your point of view on the value of education: education is the key to developing a society, so it must be taken seriously."

CHINESE

Bo: "**在某种程度上，我知道我会在**图书馆里找到你。"

Mei: "**我必**须在这里。为了额外的学分，我报名参加了一个应用程序开发课程，这意味着我必须通过一个名为"应用程序开发原则"**的推荐文本，并在本周**进行测试。"

Bo: "**我知道，**这对你有好处。**但是我**厌倦了上学，而且我很可能不去上一堂课。"

Mei: "**我**们不再上高中了；**每一课都必须认真对待。**"

Bo: "还是什么？"

Mei: "这不明显吗？**或者你会失**败。"

Bo: "**老实说，我更喜欢经营家族企业，但我的父亲坚持认为我必须先完成学业。当代大学教育**对我来说不是很重要，所以我真的不怕F。"

Mei: "**我明白你的来源，但我不同意你**对教育价值的看法：教育是发展社会的关键，所以必须认真对待。"

第十二章

不正当行为

关键词: Stop, forget, take, listen, speak, change, shut up, do, look, write, send.

走	Go
想象一下你是对的	Imagine that you are right
不要发出太大的噪音	Do not make so much noise
不要在我的订单前拍摄	Do not shoot before my order
把这个问题视为一个机会	Look at this issue as an opportunity
我们走吧	Let's walk
不要开枪	Don't shoot
更换光盘	Change the disc
做三明治	Make the sandwiches
想象一下，你已经二十岁了	Imagine that you are twenty years old
去公园	Go to the park
我们做个沙拉吧	Let's make a salad
把小说放在桌子上	Put the novel on the table
选择其中一个	Choose one or the other
随时随地来	Come whenever you want
看看你做了什么	Look what you did
向他们发送计划内容	Send them what was planned
忘了那个女孩	Forget that girl
让我解释	Let me explain

今晚给我发消息	Send me a message tonight
看下一页	Look at the next page
不要来这里	Do not come here
戴上你儿子的帽子	Put on your hat my son
选择一个盘子	Choose a plate
请让我们说一句	Please let us say a last word

训练时间

停止	Stop
不要不开心	Don't be unhappy
少吃面包	Eat less bread
听听你自己	Listen to yourself
我们来喝茶吧	Let's drink tea
跑，你迟到了	Run, you are late
前进十步	Go forward ten steps
吃草莓	Eat the strawberries
让我们坚强	Let's be strong
听我的朋友	Listen my friend
我的儿子，喝你的牛奶	Drink your milk, my son
别这样看着我	Stop looking at me like that
继续，灯是绿色的	Go on, the light is green
我说话时保持安静	Be quiet when I speak
把那纸给我	Give me that paper
拿走属于你的东西	Take what belongs to you
在这里写下您的地址	Write your address here
告诉我，你恋爱了吗？	Tell me, are you in love?
请原谅我们迟到了	Excuse us for being late

故事模式

ENGLISH

Ma: "Excuse me, I missed the first train and I had to catch another one, besides, I do not think the first five minutes count a lot".

Zhu: "Next time, I'll start alone."

Ma: "I understand, I'll compensate you."

Zhu: "Definitely, choose from this list and tell me how you want to start."

1. Wash our dishes for a week.

2. Remain silent for one hour.

3. Write an essay that explains why you will never be late again.

4. Buy me The Simple Way To Learn Spanish, volume two.

5. Forget about television for a week.

6. Run three times a week with me.

7. Give me all your monthly income.

8. Send me a text message that says 'Hi, I love you' every day, until the end of the month.

9. Let me play all your free throws every time you play NBA with Patrick.

CHINESE

Ma: "对不起,我错过了第一班火车,我不得不赶上另一辆火车,此外,我不认为前五分钟计算很多"。

Zhu: "下次,我会独自一人。"

Ma: "我明白了,我会赔偿你的。"

Zhu: "当然,请从这个清单中选择并告诉我你想如何开始。"

把我们的菜洗净一个星期。

2.保持沉默一小时。

写一篇文章,解释为什么你再也不会迟到。

给我买简单的学习西班牙语的方法,第二卷。

忘了电视一个星期。

6.和我一起跑三次。

7.把你所有的月收入给我。

8.每天给我发一条短信"嗨,我爱你",直到月底。

9.每次和帕特里克一起打NBA,让我全部罚球。

第十三章

科学

关键词: Technology, titles, calculations, invention, analysis, formula, research, matter, theory.

圈子	The circle
气氛	The atmosphere
我发现了一个	I made a discovery
我在线	I am online
原料很少见	The raw material is rare
搜索是全球性的	The search is global
这不是我的强项	It is not my strong point
能量来自太阳	The energy comes from the sun
理论上，是的	In theory, Yes
该设备的功能很简单	The function of this equipment is simple
线条怎么样？	How are the lines?
我有一件黑白点的衬衫	I have a shirt with black and white dots
这是一种大量的能量	This is a large quantity of energy
我喜欢物理科学	I like the physical sciences
你可以解释一下这个公式	You can explain the formula
她开始分析	She starts the analysis
我不喜欢你的方法	I do not like your methods
他们的分析很好	Their analyses are good
科学很重要	Science is important
该方法具有两个优点	This method offers two advantages

它是这种药的配方	It is the formula of this medicine
科学并不完美	Science is not perfect
分析分两个阶段进行	The analysis is done in two stages

训练时间

温度下降	The temperature drops
这是一个规模问题	It is a question of scale
圆圈是红色的	The circle is red
科学家	The scientist
她知道自己的极限	She knows her limits
今晚是三度	It is three degrees this evening
这不是一项发明	It is not an invention
我必须知道	I must know it
圆的半径	The radius of the circle
他不喜欢数学	He does not like mathematics

故事模式

ENGLISH

J.D Moneyfella: "Is it going to work this time? It does not seem possible to me."

Professor Makkonen: "To a certain extent, yes."

J.D Moneyfella: "And do you believe that your invention will help to reach it?"

Professor Makkonen: "Sir, nothing is impossible with science, I think we have the right technology now, according to my calculations, we will also need raw materials, as described in the research paper."

J.D Moneyfella: "I do not doubt the extent of your knowledge, but so far, all we have done is circulate the problem. We are where we started. At this point, it is safe to say that there are limits to our understanding of the subject, even for you."

Professor Makkonen: "On the contrary, sir, this formula suggests that there could be many other ways to explore it."

J.D Moneyfella: "Mathematics does not interest me, Professor, it will never be the case."

CHINESE

J.D Moneyfella: "这次会起作用吗？ 这对我来说似乎不太可能。"

Professor Makkonen: "**在某种程度上，是的。**"

J.D Moneyfella: "**你相信你的**发明有助于达到它吗？"

Professor Makkonen: "**先生，科学没有什么是不可能的，我**认为我们现在拥有合适的技术，根据我的计算，我们还需要原材料，如研究论文所述。"

J.D Moneyfella: "**我不**怀疑你的知识程度，但到目前为止，我们所做的只是传播问题。 我们是我们开始的地方。 在这一点上，可以肯定地说，即使对你来说，我们对这个主题的理解也是有限的。"

Professor Makkonen: "**相反， 先生，**这个公式表明可能还有很多方法可以探索它。"

J.D Moneyfella: "**数学**对我不感兴趣，教授，情况永远不会如此。"

第十四章

运输

关键词: Flight, bus, ticket, passport, passengers, station, accident, acceleration, driving, airport, metro, plane, motorcycle, train, travel, engine, boat.

公交车	The bus
出租车	The taxi
车站	The station
那个飞机	The airplane
火车	The train
摩托车	The motorcycle
导游	The guide
地铁	The subway
电机	The motor
一个机场	An airport
护照	The passport
旅行愉快	Have a good trip
船沿河而下	The boat goes down the river
这列火车在哪里？	Where is this train going?
这辆车有一个新发动机	The car has a new engine
去伦敦的火车在哪里？	Where is the train to London?
三类船	Three classes of boats
车站在哪？	Where is the station?
这次旅行很长？	The trip is long?
湖上有几艘船	A few boats are on the lake
我飞	I fly

你知道怎么开车吗？	Do you know how to drive?
我的翅膀在哪里？	Where are my wings
摩托车是黄色的	The motorcycle is yellow
我从机场步行	I walk from the airport
我的飞机飞往法国	My plane is flying to France
敌人飞过景观	The enemies fly over the landscape
我喜欢非洲的气候	I like the African climate
亚洲是一个大陆	Asia is a continent

训练时间

我说西班牙语	I speak Spanish
汽油是我的车	The petrol is for my car
一辆汽车有一个方向盘	A car has a steering wheel
这是一张免费门票	It is a free ticket
去釜山的巴士在哪里？	Where is the bus to Busan?
这位女士说法语	The woman speaks French
改变你的汽车轮胎！	Change the tire of your car!
游客参观博物馆	The tourists visit the museum
他们是公共汽车的乘客	They are the passengers of the bus
你不去看我	You do not visit me
你有护照吗？	Do you have your passport
游客有一个蓝色的手提箱	The tourist has a blue suitcase
意大利人在晚餐时喝葡萄酒	Italians drink wine with their dinner

我们是乘客	We are the passengers
他在开车	He is driving
你的旅程从这里开始	Your journey starts here
护士正在停车	The nurse is parking her car
他发生车祸	He has a car accident
由于交通，我们迟到了	We were late because of the traffic
从什么时候开车？	Since when do we drive?
那么，我们加速还是放慢？	So, do we speed up or slow down?
你不在这个世界上	You are not in this world
我很快	I am fast
这是直达列车吗？	Is it a direct train?
在这里加速是危险的	It is dangerous to accelerate here
当灯光呈橙色时，你必须放慢速度	You have to slow down when the light is orange
我们一直很快	We have been fast

故事模式

ENGLISH

Chun: "What are you doing with the car keys?"

Bo: "I want to change the tires of the car and examine the engine. My brother and I will go to Marseille Provence airport later today."

Chun: "Where are you travelling to?"

Bo: "Caen."

Chun: "Why do you need a flight? it will take only a few hours of driving. Transportation is cheaper by road than by plane, unless you just want to burn francs."

Bo: "I know this. Ideally, I would have liked to go on my bike, or bus, but the traffic is very difficult in the morning, and I would like to get there sooner. In addition, like other passengers on board, I can afford it."

Chun: "I think it's a waste of money. I used to fly to London from Italy frequently, but I would never have spent such an amount at a distance like this. If it's the speed and the price you prefer, I'll say go with the trains."

Bo: "I'm tempted not to take your advice after what happened with the exams, but you've always delivered, and I personally love trains. Especially the Eurostar trains."

CHINESE

Chun: "你在用车钥匙做什么？"

Bo: "我想改变汽车轮胎并检查发动机。我哥哥和我今天晚些时候将前往马赛普罗旺斯机场。"

Chun: "你要去哪儿？"

Bo: "卡昂。"

Chun: "你为什么需要飞机？只需几个小时的驾驶时间。除非你只想燃烧法郎，否则交通便宜于公路而非飞机。"

Bo: "我知道这一点。理想情况下，我本来喜欢骑自行车或公共汽车，但早上的交通非常困难，我希望能早点到达那里。此外，和其他乘客一样，我买得起。"

Chun: "我认为这是浪费金钱。我曾经经常从意大利飞往伦敦，但我永远不会在这样的距离上花这么多钱。如果这是你喜欢的速度和价格，我会说跟火车一起去吧。"

Bo: "我很想在考试结束后不接受你的建议，但是你总是交付，我个人喜欢火车。尤其是欧洲之星列车。"

第十五章

经济学

关键词: Boss, investment, banking, market, salary, employment, cash, consumers, workers, factory.

现金	**Cash**
Marko是我们的经理	**Marko is our manager**
他们是手工工人	They came as manual workers
她从事旅游业	**She works in tourism**
这些车很经济	These cars are economical
多少钱？	**What is the price?**
她有一个银行账户	**She has a bank account**
鱼类消费依然强劲	Fish consumption is still strong
我们从这次经历中获益	We have profited from this experience
这对作家来说是一个很好的奖励	That is a good prize for the writer
我们这里没有女工	We do not have female workers here
这家公司赚了很多钱	This company makes a lot of profit
这是该行业的重要合同	It is an important contract for that industry
此产品可供出售	This product is for sale
这位先生有很多资金	This gentleman has a lot of capital
我的叔叔是一名雇员	**My uncle is an employee**
工人们正在制造汽车	The workers are going to build cars
这是找你的零钱	Here is your change
我写合同	**I write the contracts**

销售额正在增加	Sales are increasing
快乐的员工是优秀的员工	Happy employees are good employees
所有这些行业现在已经消失了	All those industries have now disappeared
这些女士是模范员工	These ladies are model employees
我们要赚钱	We are going to make profits
我想租一辆车	I would like to rent a car
她收到了不错的薪水	She receives a good salary
我们必须减少消费	We must consume less

训练时间

工业设计	Industrial design
巴黎证券交易所	The Paris Stock Exchange
我们有一个房间出租	We have one room for rent
利润很小	The profit is small
他在证券交易所工作	He works at the stock exchange
他的工资是我的两倍	He earns twice my salary
这是一个工业城市	This is an industrial city
我们要赚钱	We are going to make profits
工资在月底支付	Salaries are paid at the end of the month
好处很小	The benefit is small
我的信用卡在哪里？	Where is my credit card?
我找到了一份工作	I have a job for you
工会是全国性的	The union is national

她正在招人	She is hiring people
她有巨大的财富	She has an enormous fortune
老板雇佣工人	The boss employs workers
竞争既不纯粹也不完美	Competition is neither pure nor perfect
工会知道这一点	The unions know it
她有三笔贷款支付她的房子	She has three loans to pay for her house
我们特别在春天雇用	We hire especially in the spring
老板是工厂的老板	The boss is the owner of the factory
价格在账单上	The price is on the bill
这是我的订单	It is my order
那些消费者很富有	Those consumers are rich
你看市场	You see the markets

训练时间

这是一项重要的投资	It is an important investment
这家公司的管理很困难	The management of this company is difficult
市场要求更多	The market asks for more
消费者是王道	The consumer is king
然而，他们的主人是美国人	Nevertheless, their owner is American
你的东西在哪里？	Where are your things?
服务包括在内	Service is included
我必须接受他的提议	I have to accept his offer
这是他们的广告	It is in their advertising

投资正在下降	The investments are falling
咖啡的生产在这个国家很重要	The production of coffee is important in this country
她正在出差	She is making a business trip
她正在为法国的秘密服务工作	She is working for the French secret services
这是一个很好的协议	It is a good deal
这项生产需要三到四个月	That production takes between three and four months
门票花费一百欧元	The ticket costs a hundred euros
这件外套价格昂贵但价格实惠	The coat is expensive but it is worth its price
它的确切价值是多少？	What is its exact value?
我的口袋里有五块钱	I have five dollars in my pocket
这是一个可爱的黑色皮革钱包	It is a lovely black leather purse
这是一美元	This is a dollar
但是，它太贵了	However, it is too expensive
这需要时间，但结果值得付出努力	It takes time, but the results are worth the effort
我的鞋很贵	My shoes are expensive
女士的帽子很贵	The women's hats are expensive
你有更便宜的汽车吗？	Do you have cheaper cars?
她有八十欧元	She has eighty euros
友谊是一个坚实的价值	Friendship is a solid value

我的口袋里有十一欧元 — I have eleven euros in my pocket

那张照片价值数百万 — That photo is worth millions

左栏是空的 — The left column is empty

他经营一家公司 — He runs a company

我的堂兄失业了 — My cousin is unemployed

这个部门正在增长 — This sector is growing

你有现金吗？ — Do you have cash?

这个比率高于全国税率 — This rate is above the national rate

我有十家不同的公司 — I have ten different companies

该表包含四列和八行 — The table contains four columns and eight rows

故事模式

ENGLISH

Mr. Harcourt: "Here is your money, keep the change."

Ming: "Thank you, Mr. Harcourt, it's quite generous, but it exceeds my initial cost."

Mr. Harcourt: "Do not bother, I loved your job and I saw your car outside, in this economy, we need all the help we can, consider it a small loan."

Ming: "I am very grateful, sir, I knew it was an important investment for you and I had to give the best of myself."

Mr. Harcourt: "I know, that's why I have another job for you, if you're interested."

Ming: "Everything for the boss, I'm all ears."

Mr. Harcourt: "All the details are in this file: the room is for rent, the product is for sale and the prices are indicated on the invoice, what I just paid you is the salary offered if you accept work."

Ming: "Thank you for the offer sir, but it's too much for me, and I'm not sure I can handle three jobs, but I have a cousin who is often unemployed. He is currently working in a factory near the city."

CHINESE

Mr. Harcourt: "这是你的钱,保持变化。"

Ming: "谢谢你,哈考特先生,这很慷慨,但是它超过了我的初始成本。"

Mr. Harcourt: "**不要打扰**,我喜欢你的工作,我看到你的车在外面,在这个经济环境中,我们需要所有的帮助,我们可以认为这是一笔小额贷款。"

Ming: "**我非常感激, 先生, 我知道**这对你来说是一项重要的投资,我必须尽我所能。"

Mr. Harcourt: "**我知道,** 这就是为什么我有另一份工作,如果你有兴趣的话。"

Ming: "**老板的一切, 我都是耳朵。**"

Mr. Harcourt: "**所有**细节都在这个文件中:房间是出租,产品是出售,价格在发票上注明,我刚给你的是你接受工作时提供的工资。"

Ming: "谢谢你的提议先生,但这对我来说太过分了,而且我不确定我能处理三份工作,但我有一个经常失业的堂兄。 **他目前在该市附近的一家工厂工作。**"

第十六章

体育

关键词: Strike, ball, stadiums, sport, equipment, gym, champion, run, player, swim, golf, coach, goal, leisure.

球	The ball
玩家;选手	The player
目标	The goal
运动	The sport
团队	The teams
一个团队	A team
一辆自行车	A bicycle
舞蹈	Dance
我击球了	I hit the ball
今晚不要去体育场	Do not go to the stadium tonight
他们喜欢跑步	They like running
她打红球	She hits the red ball
我喜欢运动	I like sports
我们的女儿上舞蹈课	Our daughter takes dance lessons
我在体育场	I am at the stadium
这是一个球	It is a ball
他让我们游泳	He lets us swim
他在踢足球	He is playing soccer
我的朋友让她的儿子跑了	My friend lets her son run
他是法国的冠军	He is champion of France
自行车是新的	The bicycles are new

所有的球员都在那里	All the players were there
这支球队有很好的球员	This team has good players
我哥哥正在使用那辆自行车	My brother is using that bicycle
他是一个糟糕的球员吗？	Is he a bad player?
明知道如何游泳	Ming knows how to swim

训练时间

他的父亲不打高尔夫球	His father does not play golf
他们在体育馆玩耍	They play in the gymnasium
比赛很简单	The match has been easy
你不打网球？	You do not play tennis?
我们输了比赛	We lost the competition
你的爱好是什么？	What are your hobbies?
这是一场足球比赛	It is a football
看鸟是一个很好的爱好	Watching birds is a nice hobby
他有球	He has the ball
他们在健身房吗？	Are they at the gym?
他打高尔夫球	He plays golf
我去散步了	I went for a walk
我不可能打败	I am impossible to beat
他们打进一球	They have scored a goal
我不得不丢球	I have to throw the ball
我是你的教练	I am your coach
好球	Nice shot

故事模式

ENGLISH

Bo: "Hello Shen, how are you today, you look very lively."

Shen: "Not bad actually, I'm very excited for the match, I can not wait for the kickoff, and you?"

Bo: "In truth, I do not know anything about football, I only know Messi and Ronaldo, the only ball sport I can play is golf, and I'm just trying to get an extra hobby by coming here today."

Shen: "It's surprising, I never would have guessed, by the way, how are you in shape? I've never seen you at the gym."

Bo: "It's easy, these days, I go to school with my bike instead of my car, I swim, I run and I walk in the evening when the weather is nice."

Shen: "I see, if anyone asks, France is the current world champion of football, and this stadium is called the Allianz Arena.

In addition, the match takes place between two teams, Bayern Munich and Borussia Dortmund. We will support Bayern. They are the reds."

Bo: "Is the other team good?"

Shen: "They are really hard to beat, thanks to their new coach and their new tactics."

CHINESE

Bo: "**你好沉，你今天好**吗，你看起来很活泼。"

Shen: "实际上还不错，我对这场比赛感到非常兴奋，我等不及开球了，你呢？"

Bo: "事实上，我对足球一无**所知，我只知道梅西和**罗纳尔多，我能打的唯一一项球类运动就是打高尔夫球，我只是想通过今天来这里来获得额外的爱好。"

Shen: "这是令人惊讶的，顺便说一下，我从来没有想过，你是怎么形状的？我从来没有在健身房见过你。"

Bo: "这很容易，这些天，我带着自行车而不是我的车上学，游泳，跑步，晚上天气好的时候我会走路。"

Shen: "**我看，如果有人问**，法国是现在的世界足球冠军，这个体育场叫做安联球场。

此外，比赛将在两支球队之间进行，拜仁慕尼黑和多特蒙德队。我们将支持拜仁。他们是红人。"

Bo: "**其他球**队好吗？"

Shen: "**由于他们**的新教练和他们的新战术，他们真的很难被击败。"

第十七章

精神

关键词: Spirit, gods, ghosts.

哲学	The philosophy
教堂	The churches
神圣的灵魂	The holy spirit
神	Gods
天哪！	My God!
死后有生命吗？	Is there life after death?
你有一个美丽的心灵	You have a beautiful mind
她没有宗教信仰	She has no religion
我有信心	I had faith
她的灵魂在天堂	Her soul is in heaven
你是个天使	You are an angel
感谢上帝	Thank God
没人能避免死亡	Nobody can avoid death
我相信你	I have faith in you
你相信什么宗教？	What is your religion?
他不虔诚	He is not religious
我们可以期待什么？	What can we hope for?
天堂在哪里？	Where is heaven?
他会下地狱	He is going to hell
她相信鬼魂	She believes in ghosts
这是一个神圣的对象	It is a holy object
她会下地狱	She will go to hell
这是教堂之城	It is the city of churches
这是一个可爱的教堂	It is a lovely church

故事模式

ENGLISH

"May his soul rest in perfect peace." said the preacher.

"You see my dear brothers, no matter how intelligent, strong, handsome or rich, the truth is that we will all face death when our time comes.

The question then becomes 'Where do you think you will end up after death?' For those of us who belong to the Christian religion, we trust in the grace of our Lord and Savior, Jesus Christ.

We believe he will lead us to heaven when we die, as long as we embody his heavenly values, and keep the commandments of his father, our father, Jehovah. Others believe in reincarnation, or the idea that we return to this world in another body after death."

"My God, Lucas, let's respect the dead, stop playing with your phone and listen to the preacher!" said the elderly lady in a silent tone.

"Oh, Madame Valeria, I'm sure the deceased's ghost would not bother me if I checked some emails." Lucas replied, his eyes still stuck on the phone screen.

"You speak like a pagan." said Madame Valeria.

CHINESE

"愿他的灵魂安息吧。"传教士说道。

"你看到我亲爱的兄弟们,无论多么聪明,坚强,英俊或富有,事实是,当我们的时间到来时,我们都将面临死亡。

那么问题就变成了"你认为你死后会在哪里结束?"对于我们这些属于基督教的人,我们相信我们的主和救主耶稣基督的恩典。

只要我们体现他的天上价值观,并遵守他父亲,我们的父亲,耶和华的诫命,我们相信他会在我们死后将我们带到天堂。其他人相信转世,或者说我们死后会在另一个身体中回归这个世界的想法。"

"我的上帝,卢卡斯,让我们尊重死者,停止玩你的手机,听听传教士的声音!"老太太沉默地说道。

"哦,瓦莱里亚夫人,我确定如果我检查了一些电子邮件,死者的鬼魂不会打扰我。"卢卡斯回答说,他的眼睛仍然卡在电话屏幕上。

"你说的像个异教徒。"瓦莱里娅夫人说。

第18章

调情

关键词: Lovely, warm, go out, model, like.

你叫什么名字？	**What's your name?**
我喜欢你	**I like you**
你是模特儿吗？	**Are you a model?**
你经常来这儿吗？	**You come here often?**
你想要和我一起跳舞吗？	**Do you want to dance with me?**
我们要到你的地方还是我的地方？	**Are we going to your place or mine?**
你好！白马王子	**Hello! Prince Charming**
你想和我一起出去吗？	**Do you want to go out with me?**
我能请你喝一杯么？	**Can I buy you a drink?**
你想去喝一杯吗？	**Would you like to go get a drink?**
你好，美女	**Hello beautiful**
它在这里很热，还是仅仅是你？	**Is it hot in here, or is that just you?**

故事模式

ENGLISH

Ma: "I like the way this dress looks on you, are you a model?"

Liz: "Unfortunately, no, but I can be a model if you prefer."

Ma: "I think I already like you."

Liz: "Thanks, I think I like you too."

Ma: "That's great, can I buy you a drink then?"

Liz: "Of course, go for it."

* Two glasses of tequila are ordered *

Ma: "So what's your name?"

Liz: "Liz."

Ma: "Nice to meet you Elizabeth, do you come here often?"

Liz: "Not really, and its really Melissa or Melissande in full, but I'm fine, I guess."

Ma: "Forgive my mistake ... Maybe I was just confused by your beautiful smile, do you want to dance with me Liz?"

Liz: "I would, but I'm not really a great dancer, and hip hop is not really my kind of music, I like electronic music."

CHINESE

Ma: "我喜欢这件衣服在你身上的样子,你是模特吗?"

Liz: "不幸的是,不,但如果你愿意,我可以成为一名模特。"

Ma: "我想我已经喜欢你了。"

Liz: "谢谢,我想我也喜欢你。"

Ma: "那很好,我可以给你买一杯饮料吗?"

Liz: "当然,去吧。"

订购两杯龙舌兰酒

Ma: "你叫什么名字?"

Liz: "莉兹。"

Ma: "很高兴认识你,伊丽莎白,你经常来这里吗?"

Liz: "不是真的,而且它真的是Melissa或Melissande,但我想,我很好。"

Ma: "请原谅我的错误……也许我只是被你美丽的笑容迷惑了,你想和我一起跳舞吗?"

Liz: "我愿意,但我不是一个伟大的舞者,嘻哈不是真正的音乐,我喜欢电子音乐。"

第十九章

身份

关键词: Eggs, always, saves, things, must, them, two.

没有什么可以天长地久	Nothing lasts forever
来得便当去得快	Easy come, easy go
甚至没有伤到我	Did not even hurt me
眼不见，心不烦	Out of sight, out of mind
另一边的草总是更绿	The grass is always greener on the other side
她将用手指在鼻子里赢得胜利	She is going to win with her fingers in her nose
这个孩子不知道如何抓住他的舌头	This child does not know how to hold his tongue
没有太多的酒，只请一滴	Not too much wine, only a drop please
再次，关闭	On again, Off again
在罗马做到入乡随俗	When in Rome, do as the Romans do
一切美好的事情都会结束	All good things come to an end
乞丐不能选择	The early bird catches the worm
欲速则不达	Beggars cant be choosers
乞丐不能选择	Haste makes waste
你只活一次	You only live once
墙壁有耳朵	The walls have ears
对每一个他自己	To each his own
在我的尸体上	Over my dead body
你不能吃你的蛋糕也没有	You can't eat your cake and have it too

故事模式

ENGLISH

Chun: "Hi."

Mei: "Hi, how's your day?"

Chun: "Pretty good. What are you reading?"

Mei: "This is a list of my top ten favorite idioms, in no particular order."

1. "Nobody tells a blind man that it's raining."

2. "When the cat is out, the mice will play."

3. "Make hay while the sun is shining."

4. "Those who need babies, will not go to sleep with socks."

5. "Stupid flies are buried with the corpse."

6. "At the beginning of the bed, early to go up."

7. "When in France, do as the French do."

8. "We only live once."

9. "Hope is eternal."

10. "All good things come to an end."

CHINESE

Chun: "嗨。"

Mei: "嗨,你今天过得怎么样?"

Chun: "挺好的。 你在读什么?"

Mei: "这是我最喜欢的十大成语列表,没有特别的顺序。"

"没有人告诉一个盲人正在下雨。"

"当猫出门时,老鼠会玩。"

"在阳光明媚的时候制作干草。"

"那些需要婴儿的人,不会带着袜子去睡觉。"

"愚蠢的苍蝇被尸体埋葬了。"

6."在床的开头,早点上去。"

"在法国的时候,就像法国人一样。"

"我们只活一次。"

9."希望是永恒的。"

10."所有美好事物都将结束。"

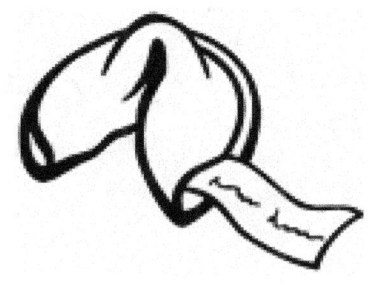

END OF BOOK TWO

For the complete experience, please get the other books in the series.

#THESIMPLEWAYTOLEARNSPANISH

For updates on the next book, or if you'd just like to discuss this one, we're available on twitter as the @BadCreativ3, and on facebook www.facebook.com/BadCreativ3

OTHER BADCREATIVE BOOKS

The Simple Way To Learn French

The Simple Way To Learn Spanish

The Simple Way To Learn Portoguese

Thank you for reading, and we hope you would be kind enough to give us a review on our amazon page.

www.ingramcontent.com/pod-product-compliance
Lightning Source LLC
Chambersburg PA
CBHW052110110526
44592CB00013B/1548